INVESTIGATING THE UNEXPLAINED

ATLANTIS

BY PAIGE V. POLINSKY

BELLWETHER MEDIA • MINNEAPOLIS, MN

Blastoff! Discovery launches
a new mission: reading to learn.
Filled with facts and features, each
book offers you an exciting new
world to explore!

This edition first published in 2020 by Bellwether Media, Inc.

No part of this publication may be reproduced in whole or in
part without written permission of the publisher.
For information regarding permission, write to
Bellwether Media, Inc., Attention: Permissions Department,
6012 Blue Circle Drive, Minnetonka, MN 55343.

Library of Congress Cataloging-in-Publication Data

Names: Polinsky, Paige V., author.
Title: Atlantis / by Paige V. Polinsky.
Description: Minneapolis, MN : Bellwether Media, Inc., 2020.
 | Series: Blastoff! Discovery : Investigating the Unexplained
 | Includes bibliographical references and index.
Identifiers: LCCN 2019000959 (print) | LCCN 2019015867
 (ebook) | ISBN 9781618915795 (ebook) |
 ISBN 9781644870389 (hardcover : alk. paper)
Subjects: LCSH: Atlantis (Legendary place)–Juvenile literature.
Classification: LCC GN751 (ebook) | LCC GN751 .P65 2020
 (print) | DDC   001.94–dc23
LC record available at https://lccn.loc.gov/2019000959

Editor: Kate Moening   Designer: Andrea Schneider

Printed in the United States of America, North Mankato, MN.

TABLE OF CONTENTS

SECRET IN THE SAND

Leo shuffles along the bottom of the Mediterranean Sea. Sofia said the **magnetometer** showed something strange in this area. All Leo sees is sand, rocks, and fish. But he will search for hours if that means finding the ruins of Atlantis!

Suddenly, Sofia radios from their ship. "Hey, wait! What's that to your left?" Leo turns. The light from his diving suit brightens the water. Its beam lands on a strange lump in the sand.

REC

"Moving in for a closer look," Leo says. He carefully pulls a flat, round disk from the seafloor. It looks like it is made of stone, but a small chip reveals metal shining underneath.

"Wow. Nice find!" Sofia says. "Ready to surface?"

"Yeah. I want to get a date on this."

A cable tugs at Leo's suit. As it pulls him up through the water, he stares down at the disk. Is this a clue? Has he finally found proof of the lost city of Atlantis?

A LASTING LEGEND

Legends of Atlantis began with the Greek **philosopher** Plato around 360 BCE. Plato wrote that Atlantis existed about 9,000 years earlier. Its people were wealthy but grew greedy. They angered their gods by attacking other lands. The gods helped the Greek city of Athens defeat Atlantis. Then, the gods destroyed Atlantis with floods and **earthquakes**.

Athens today

TREASURE ISLAND

According to Plato, Atlantis was nearly perfect. The beautiful island was rich with wood and metal. Plato said its people were children of the god Poseidon. These half-gods were experts at sailing and building ships.

GREECE

Europe

Asia

Aegean
Sea

Athens

Mediterranean Sea

Santorini

Atlantis does not appear on trusted ancient maps. Some people say it never existed. But others believe the city was real. They say Atlantis is still hidden somewhere, waiting to be discovered!

SEEKING THE LOST CITY

People thought Atlantis was a legend for centuries. But in the 1400s, European explorers began sailing across the Atlantic Ocean. As they found unknown lands, people turned back to Plato's stories. Was Atlantis out there too?

Ignatius Donnelly

CURIOUS CLAIMS

Donnelly's work stirred much interest in Atlantis. People made wild claims about the legend! Some said they had secret writings from Atlantis. Others said Atlanteans used magic crystals to build their city!

Some **Atlantologists** thought the island was sunken in the eastern Atlantic. In 1882, a man named Ignatius Donnelly wrote a book about it. He claimed every society originally came from Atlantis. **Skeptics** found many mistakes, but the book was a smash hit. The search for Atlantis was on!

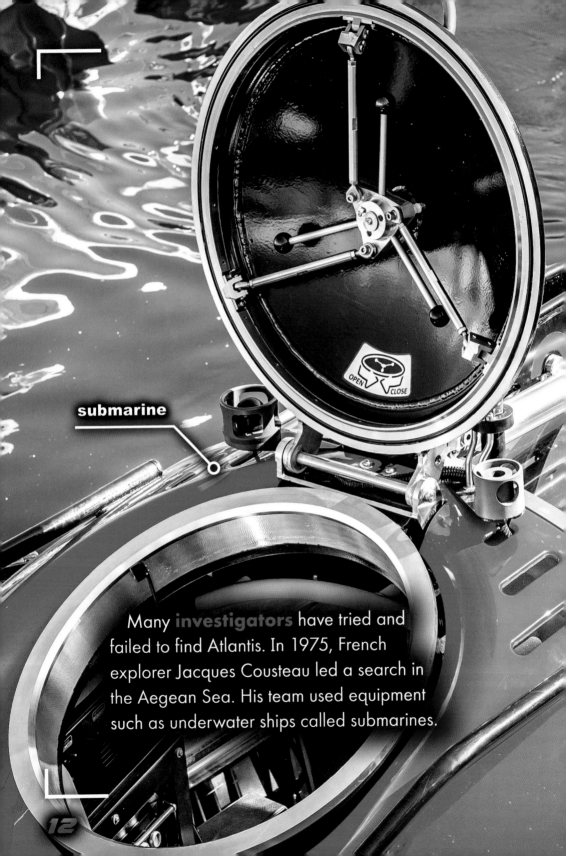

submarine

Many **investigators** have tried and failed to find Atlantis. In 1975, French explorer Jacques Cousteau led a search in the Aegean Sea. His team used equipment such as underwater ships called submarines.

HÜBNER'S MAJOR CLUES

Hübner's computer program used 51 clues from Plato's writings, including:

 The city is near the sea

 Elephants live in the area

 There are mountains to the north

 Rings of land and water surround the city

 The city is built with red, black, and white stone

Not all researchers dove beneath the waves. In the early 2000s, Michael Hübner collected clues from Plato's writings. He used a computer to study 400 real places for matching features. Morocco's Souss-Massa plain matched the most clues! Hübner believed the wave that destroyed Atlantis washed the city to sea. This remains a strong explanation.

HOW GROUND-PENETRATING RADAR WORKS

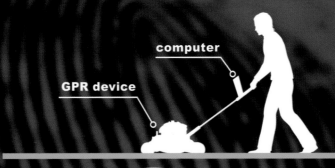

computer

GPR device

returning—○ radio signals

outgoing radio signals

object—○

1. The GPR device sends radio signals into the ground.

2. If the signals hit an object, they bounce back to the device.

3. A computer measures the time it takes for the signals to return.

4. The signals' travel time tells researchers the depth and location of the object.

satellite image

DIVING WITH THE STARS

Freund worked with famous filmmaker James Cameron during the 2016 investigation. Cameron turned their experience into a movie, *Atlantis Rising*. But he is best known for his movies *Titanic* and *Avatar*.

In 2004, **satellite images** led Spanish scientists to a site near Cadiz, Spain. American professor Richard Freund thought they might find Atlantis. He joined their team in 2009. Using **ground-penetrating radar** (GPR), they found real ruins! But Freund could not prove they came from Atlantis.

In 2016, Freund joined two filmmakers on another investigation. They searched the Atlantic and the Mediterranean. Their crew found six anchors from the **Bronze Age**! These may have belonged to an Atlantean harbor. However, more proof is needed.

illustration of Atlantis's rings of land and water

PROFILE:
THE CADIZ INVESTIGATION

The 2004 satellite images led scientists to a marsh outside of Cadiz. In 2009, Atlantologist Richard Freund brought new tools to the team. They studied the marsh with GPR and **digital mapping**. Using divers and **sonar**, they searched the coast for sunken **artifacts**.

In 2011, the investigators found 2,800-year-old ruins! They also discovered ruins in central Spain. Freund called these "memorial cities." He believed they were built by people who escaped Atlantis. The Spanish researchers disagreed. They said the ruins were too young.

BIRD'S-EYE VIEW

Satellite images allow researchers to view areas all over the world! Photos taken from above a site can reveal clues that are otherwise hidden. This is helpful when selecting a place to investigate.

divers using sonar

Doñana National Park, where the Cadiz research team worked

THE SEARCH IS ON

Most Atlantologists agree the ancient city is buried out of sight. They must use advanced tools to search for clues. Some tools use GPR to find objects hidden deep underground.

magnetometers

INVESTIGATOR TOOLBOX

magnetometer

ROV/AUV

GPR device

satellite

submarine/boat

Exosuit

Magnetometers can find buried objects, too. They sense changes in an area's **magnetic field**. These are often caused by rocks or metals. Researchers can pull a magnetometer behind a boat to track changes along the seafloor. Strange results might mean there is something hidden down below!

UNDERWATER IRON MAN

When wearing an Exosuit, a diver can stay 1,000 feet (305 meters) below the surface for up to 50 hours! The advanced suit is nicknamed the "underwater Iron Man suit."

Exosuit

Atlantologists need special gear to explore underwater sites. Early divers used simple suits with air hoses. Today's tools are more advanced! Devices called rebreathers track and manage air flow. This helps divers breathe safely while exploring the seafloor.

MAJOR ATLANTIS SEARCH SITES

Mediterranean Sea

Atlantic Ocean

4
2
1
3
5

1. **Santorini; Crete (Greece)**
2. **Cadiz (Spain)**
3. **Souss-Massa plain (Morocco)**
4. **Azores Islands (Portugal)**
5. **Bimini Islands (Bahamas)**

Advanced diving suits allow investigators to search deeper areas for longer amounts of time. These suits are very strong. Some manage divers' air supply automatically. They may also feature lights and small jets for easier movement.

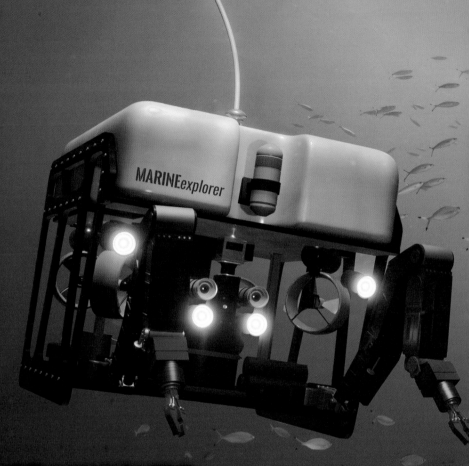

remotely operated vehicle

Even with the latest suits, diving can be dangerous.
Tools like remotely operated vehicles (ROVs)
help investigators search underwater safely.
Many ROVs have lights, video cameras, and sonar.
Cables connect an ROV to a ship. Researchers
control the robot from on board.

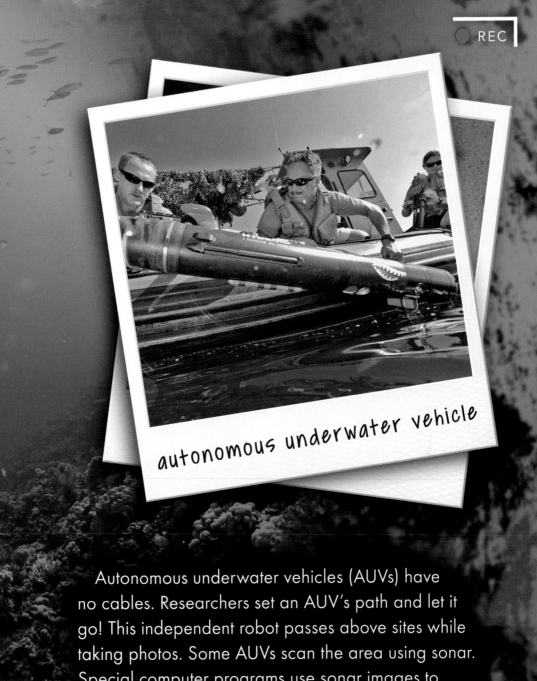

autonomous underwater vehicle

Autonomous underwater vehicles (AUVs) have no cables. Researchers set an AUV's path and let it go! This independent robot passes above sites while taking photos. Some AUVs scan the area using sonar. Special computer programs use sonar images to create a map of the seafloor.

PLATO'S PUZZLE

Most historians do not think Atlantis ever existed. They say Plato's clues do not match any real place. They also argue that there are no other records of the city being destroyed. Other people would have likely written about such a huge event.

Skeptics also point out that Plato's writings were often **allegories**. Readers cannot always take them as fact. Skeptics say the Atlantis story was probably a warning from Plato to the people of Greece. Perhaps he was trying to teach them to act wisely.

REC

Plato

volcano

Some people believe the story of Atlantis is based on true events. The island of Santorini was once home to a wealthy seafaring city. In the 1600s BCE, a volcano destroyed the city. Perhaps this became the story of Atlantis.

Santorini today

Plato said he heard the legend from other people. Maybe they changed the details before he heard the story. Maybe Plato wanted to make it more exciting. Either way, skeptics say Plato's Atlantis was a tall tale.

DIVING DEEPER

Skeptics also argue that we would have already found Atlantis if it was real. However, it is possible for ruins to hide for centuries. Scientists have discovered several sunken cities over the years.

There is little **evidence** that Atlantis exists. But researchers continue to suggest new areas to search. New technology will make these investigations more accurate. Advanced tools like AUVs will become smaller and cheaper, too. That means more people will be able to join the search. Will you dive with them?

LEGENDS COME TRUE

An Indian poem called the *Mahabharata* tells of the ancient city Dwarka. The city was swallowed up by the Arabian Sea. People thought it was a legend. But in 1963, investigators found Dwarka sunken near India's western coast. The legend was true!

GLOSSARY

allegories—stories in which the characters and events stand for ideas about human life

artifacts—items made long ago by humans

Atlantologists—people who study Atlantis

Bronze Age—the period of time that lasted from around 3000 to 1000 BCE, during which people used bronze to make weapons and tools

digital mapping—the process of using data to create a computer image of a particular area

earthquakes—disasters in which the ground shakes from the movement of Earth's crust

evidence—information that helps prove or disprove something

ground-penetrating radar—a system that uses radio waves to find and track objects underground

investigators—people who try to find out the facts about things in order to learn if or how they happened

legends—stories from the past that are believed by many people but not proven to be true

magnetic field—the area of space around a magnetic object in which magnetic forces can be detected

magnetometer—a device used to find metal objects or measure magnetic fields

philosopher—a person who studies ideas about knowledge, truth, and the meaning of life

satellite images—photos taken by a machine that orbits Earth, the moon, the sun, or a planet

skeptics—people who doubt something is true

sonar—a system that uses sound waves to detect and map objects underwater

TO LEARN MORE

AT THE LIBRARY

Hyde, Natalie. *The Lost City of Atlantis*. New York, N.Y.: Crabtree Publishing Company, 2016.

Rea, Amy C. *The Mystery of Atlantis*. Minneapolis, Minn.: Abdo Publishing, 2016.

Summers, Portia. *Was Atlantis Real?* New York, N.Y.: Enslow Publishing, 2018.

ON THE WEB

FACTSURFER

Factsurfer.com gives you a safe, fun way to find more information.

1. Go to www.factsurfer.com.

2. Enter "Atlantis" into the search box and click 🔍.

3. Select your book cover to see a list of related web sites.

INDEX

The images in this book are reproduced through the courtesy of: Zwiebackesser, front cover (Poseidon); Olive Denker, front cover (ruins); Richard Whitcombe, front cover (diver); SHIN-db, pp. 2-3, 30-32; David MG, pp. 4-5; scubadesign, pp. 6-7; Sven Hansche, pp. 8-9; Wiki Commons, pp. 10 (Ignatius Donnelly), 17 (wetlands); Algol, pp. 10-11; rfranca, pp. 10-11 (ship); NicoElNino, pp. 14-15; National Geographic Image Collection, p. 16; US Navy Photo/ Alamy, p. 17 (sonar); Marine Construction Photos/ Alamy, p. 18 (magnetometers); JackDiver, pp. 18-19; dpa picture alliance/ Alamy, pp. 20-21; Vismar UK, p. 22 (ROV); segemi, pp. 22-23 (ocean); U.S. Navy/ Wiki Commons, p. 23 (AUV); Anastasios71, pp. 24-25 (Plato); yoeml, pp. 24-25 (ruins); Guillaume Soularue/ Age Fotostock, pp. 26-27; Gyuszko-Photo, p. 27 (Santorini); Fer Gregory, pp. 28-29 (Poseidon); diversepixel,pp. 28-29 (ruins).